REFLECTIONS

JATIN SHARMA

BlueRose ONE.com
Stories Matter
NewDelhi • London

BLUEROSE PUBLISHERS
India | U.K.

BlueRose ONE.com
Stories Matter
NewDelhi • London

For permissions requests or inquiries regarding this publication, please contact:

BLUEROSE PUBLISHERS
www.BlueRoseONE.com
info@bluerosepublishers.com
+91 8882 898 898
+4407342408967

ISBN: 978-93-6783-133-5

Cover design: Yash Singhal
Typesetting: Namrata Saini

First Edition: January 2025

Verse 1

A tree stood tall amidst the forest green,
It's branches stretched and leaves serene,
Yet deep within its wooden core,
A sense of despair it could not ignore,
For though it stood among its peers,
No friend or kin to share it's story,
How it can talk skies,
To which others do not take it as glory,
How it is afraid of night and that of rain,
Which cut it apart from sandpiper's strain,
The tree shed leaves a tearful sight,
Hoping some movement in it's roots to feel some might
Still it find sheer dreams that all the wood can together sing
For its hidden eyes to shut and joy to bring
But all it see the same odd, bunch of critters wondering around
Who just sit on its branches, not the touch to which it can bound
All it, see the same visage over and over again
Oh no ! why other trees do not have brains that their roots are just like chains
And so it learned, through the years,
That solitude can bring many tears
For though, the sun may shine, bright and clear
Still loneliness is one to fear

But one day by some chance, a seed fell to the ground
And with it, hope and new life the tree found
For in its branches, a sapling grew,
A companion for the tree, so true
And so the tree found purpose and joy
In nurturing its new young boy
No longer alone it found peace
A life of solitude now did cease
No longer it talk to the skies
Further to assimilate some genuine cries
Rather it got the art; enjoying the stories of neighbouring
shrubs and even that of million flies
Its leaves started growing green
Fruits that makes every life privately sheen
Now it understand the theme of sandpiper's voice
Who after baffling in the air,
The bird comes to woods
For its soul to rejoice

Verse 2

In the light of dawn, I rose to see
A world transformed, in front of me
My clogs turned to Zeppelins in the sky
Bread from the clouds, I could not deny
Dressed in fire, I ran to hills,
My heart beating with endless thrills
But the wind shook me with fear and fright,
A destruction loomed, in the morning light
Beside me stood a man with wand in hand,
A master of fiction, in this strange land
He asked me," do you believe in black horn yarn?"
And warned me, "you should know the sound of thunder's alarm"
For in this world of wonder and awe,
Where clogs become ships and bread fall from raw
There are tales of magic and stories untold,
Where the brave and bold seek treasures of gold
And though the wind may shakes us,
And fear may take us
We must believe in the magic that surround us
I stood in the land of fire and flight
The impossible was possible with a touch of light
Boy beside me, the boy with the aircraft
Quality of flying, bird touches welkin
Boy was acting like a baskin

He asked me," do you believe in blackhorn yarn ?",
And warned me," you should better know the sound of thunder's alarm".

Verse 3

Amidst the dark and the evil air,
My heart awaits a love so fair,
For love that is strong will stand the test,
And shine on through life ' s toughest quest
True love defends, a shield embossed
But Love that is guarded tight,
Will wither away like fading light
Love can only be free,
The evergreen and everlasting tree
With hope and faith, a true friend to be
Oh !, holy, my love , my dear beloved
You are the light that keeps me covered
In the times of joy and booming glee
You catch me, cut me,set me free
For in your embrace, I find my peace,
A love that never seems to cease,
With each passing movements,
I am renewed
My heart, my soul, forever imbued
My love take my hands
Lead me through this wondrous land
Where holy love reigns supreme
And all my fears and doubts forever redeemed

Verse 4

Within the depths of my being
There lies a fiery churning sea,
Where thoughts and emotions swirl and spin
In a dance that's wild and free
Just a tongue plays with my gut
Stirring up hunger and desire,
My heart plays with my mind,
Igniting images that set my soul on fire

Like a symphony of senses
They weave a tapestry of delight,
With each note and every hue,
Filling my world with multicoloured light
But sometimes the rythm falters
And the notes become discordant
And the images that once thrilled me,
Now leave me feeling haunted
For the heart can be a fickle thing
And mind a master of deception
And when they clash and collide
They leave me lost in confusion
So I must learn to dance this dance
With grace and precision
To let my heart and mind unite
In a perfect harmonious fusion

For when they work in tandem,
They create a world that 's sublime
Where every thought and every feeling,
Is a symphony of love and time

With that, I walk through fields of green,
The air around so pure and clean,
Yet, sometimes it's hard to breathe
When the weight of my void makes me seethe

For how can one fall back and cling
To perishable personage, transient thing
When the world around is pure and bright
But still all that left is a lonely night

And when I try to speak my mind
To share my thoughts and words intwined,
Sometimes it's hard to talk at all
As people's realism makes me small

For how can one collate their heartstrings?
To perishable devil, fleeting things
When all that matters is the truth and words and deeds of honest youth
Yet, still, I walk in this path alone
With every step, a deeper tone
For In this world of purest state
Sometimes is hard to feel my fate

Verse 5

Like one at the wall of big hall
In my mind, a clock which shows time
A luxury I took for granted, a serious crime
Like a farmer who sows in spring
Thinking the harvest is his Sure thing
I talked with a river flowing to the sea,
Gave a long speech for all that could have been

Now I am left with nothing but regret
Wishing for some spirits, like fisherman's Net
But the past is gone and future I ignore in frill and vain
Leaving my eyes in race and heart in unknown pain
Ah! What a fascinating speech?
In my mind, the core of universe, it could reach
I did find it soothing to my inner ears
But never it could reach my tears

Like a villain and hero of a movie
I acted as a character, on the stage of others
No choice I could see real for my country's brothers
Because a man may choose his role to play
Things to give, things to take
Still some molds remain lunatic and terribly fake

For the normal man, it is a give and take
An equal balance, a fair shake
He takes his share, but gives in return
His place in society he shall earn

But there are those who are weak and greedy
They take and take, but they are hardly needy
Their hearts are black, their souls become dark,
Their only goal is to somehow leave their mark

And then there are divine
Whose love and grace forever shine
They give and give, with open mind and heart,
Their kindness is sheer work of art

In the ocean of yearning,
And among those who are really burning ,
There are those who are not meant to play,
The game of potential, comes their way
Their spirits are programmed to sing,
It is the beauty of bluebells to ring
In the world where hunger speaks so loud
Their silent heads stand out from the crowd
For it is the deed that is lame,
Only love and joy they aim

A serious crime, the clock shows the time
In spring, I harvested a lot,
And then tried to make the rhyme
A prison of colours,

Made my vision blind
Moments I ignored, I set the trade in my mind
Still clock shows its own,
The garden of a mysterious kind
It keep us busy all these years
All that is there and all that is here
And
In this drama, the subtle lesson of any tale we tell
True minds heal and mend in respective natures very well
For folly waits for those who rush
And wisdom lost gets harder to be brushed

Verse 6

There is a print on a marble
Like a print on my mind
Directing the fireworks through the beautiful passage
To the graceful misery
I bow down to the cool breeze near
The golden sea
I bag everything in my hands
And it is the home to see the real me
Here rest the birth
Here fails the death
It feel Mary that I cannot
Sway my mind and
With this print,
Nothing sounds immortal to the sounding birds 's wrath
For which I lose everything
Still the print describe the life
As the purpose of my breath
Hefty I ignore the times fact
My body remained my greatest fear,
Over and above the impetuous passions of my selfhood
This inadvertent peregrination
Somehow have a strong pull
Which ends me up with a print on my mind
Like a print on the marble
Directing the fireworks through the beautiful passage to the

Graceful misery
Misery that is highly subtle to sense
A mark on my chest
The imaginary is much deeper and tense
Now that I am not afraid of my mind s vast expanse
But a canvas on rent
A story of my life, tale so quaint
But the words are silly, my tongue is bent
And my voice fails, my courage is spent

And so I fear not my thought strife
But the silence that might end my life,
For a life unloved is a living strife
A tragedy that cuts as knife

Oh ! My mind is not a house of peace
Further words and thoughts cannot really teach
For a man who made a worry
sitch of a impotent mind
Smile on the face
The face is unkind
All that is real to eyes
Kills the angles behind
Why not people live their dreams
When the time is a fear less mastermind
A quirk of playing before the match
Is something, mother always reminds
Sadly the bad noise can impede the work
The work of construction in the mind
Over and above the conundrum of my speech

These hunches somehow have a strong pull
Which Presents me a print on a marble
Like a print on my mind
For joy to be attained
Better to pretend like a blind

Verse 7

A mystery oh ! Soo grand
Your thoughts, I cannot understand
Your heart, a secret you keep
But in your eyes, a promise deep
My words fall short, it seems
To reach your heart, to fulfil your dreams
But still, I must try, I must believe

Your book, story yet untold
Its pages, a treasure to unfold
I may not know what lies within
But my faith tells me to begin
I do not know what is your desire
But my feet are bound,
My heart is on fire
The enigma that astounds you,
concepts that bounds you
I must pay the price of the self
For my feet are just tied with you
A mystery soo grand
The self is not the lines on hand
Where Thoughts are like noise
All the structures, need to expand
It cannot differentiate, nor
It can tease

To understand self, we must concede
That it is not a solo bread
It is intertwined with all that
Surrounds
And in this realisation, the self is found
It cannot pick, choose and judge
For in doing so, it becomes a grudge
The self is one with everything
And in this truth, it finds its wings
So shed egos and fears
And embrace the oneness that is always here
For the self is not the self unless we see
That it is the part of everything wild and free
So all the dear hearts, listen to
A tale soo grim,
Of a served hand, a foot, a head, cut off from limb
A sight so gruesome, it make one shiver and quake
But there is a metaphor here,
A truth we must take
For just as one who serves
themselves for the fake society
Rejecting their lot, acting with impropriety,
Cut themselves off from the unity of nature s flow,
Breaking away from the path they were meant to go
Once a part of the whole, now an
Outcast alone
Am enigma lies here, sacrifices to atone
For it is open to you, to rejoin the fold
No other part has this privilege so as I am told
God s grace is upon us, not to

Be broken off from the start
And even we stand differently, we can
Still play our part
Returning to grow back to our rightful place,
A member of the whole with love and grace
So shed tears, dear heart of
Those who have served themselves, at greater cost
Hoping for god s society
Sights we have just lost
But hope remains and all can be possible
Not in any vain
For even the broken can be whole again

Verse 8

Hard to bear tears and what a grinding struggle !
How long one can smile to retain the spark
Dark and bright are meant to be immingled
oy is everywhere, in talk, in walk and even when you balk
Mostly the news from the hell
Chronicle your bear ands skitlles
Which delineate the exterior
Of the dark
Sadness is everywhere, in right, in light and even when you fight
Mostly the news from the heavens
Give you spin of disguise
Which delineate the exterior
Of the bright
The story was traumatic
With no exhibitions
With no concerns and help
The bad role speaks
Out that its hard,
The good role felt empty
And said,
It is hard to bear tears and what a grinding struggle !
How long one can cry to retain the dark
Closed eyes are the symbol of peace
Colors are meant to be released

But tears are pure,
fall down to the land of souls
Whiles eyes seeking the beauty of the scene
Another soul telling me to just stay for one day
Clock pester me to rush against the clouds
Voices all over screaming and hurting my ears
Who knows my feet slowly cry
But laughter fall down to the land of souls
Dark or bright is all I can try

Verse 9

We are not free and we do not own freedom
Power clasped by one, entice many other dumbs
We deal coins as gods of contemporary conduct of life
This magnificent damnation breaks the beauty of our minds
Stil our hunches and emotions make hard notions
Throughout the synthesis of planet earth s topography
Only humans touch the fear of mind s distortion
We talk like we pertain cherry smile
We are not a bit free to expel out from things we do not like
Is it really spartan to organise
The give and take policy of various molds ?
Why do not we have guts to play
Our desired inherited roles ?
Still seduction make workers
Seldomly few of our members
Enter the sprite world which
Generate more terror,
Terror to leave the mind of
A tinker, a giver and a product maker
Unlike monkeys in a jungle
We are not free and we do not own freedom
These yearnings for various poor powers
Make the army of witless and king without wisdom
And then sadly I felt for my seclusion
And was stuck in despair

I felt tremble in my heart
And a deadly fear then
My mind again build a roguish salesman
Like true lovers made for each other
I screamed for a perfect messenger of my kind
But the time was only incessantly
Running in my mind
In dark everything was still there
When I looked up at the sky
The star 's shine, the bird' fly
All in existence not in some other time
The very next sun
I took a walk on seaside
Every other critter, omitting people
Was talking to me in testy language
Without any past line
At sudden my heart poured with joy
Little later I cried that where we get destroyed
It is a humongous terror that some of
Our scarce faces knowingly strand themselves
In an dread and impotence
But the whole universe still
Accepts and listen to them in their real molds,
Despite of the loses they have incurred
In their social folds
It is a lie that animals and blue skies do not say' hi'
They always wanted to tell me that this is only
A thought of being alone and it is just my
Oblivion toy
Thus I am not free yet or I cannot hold the joy

Verse 10

It all started limitless years ago
The algorithm of life
With some never ending vibes
If you see with your soul and
Break it down to silence
One energy on form
Nobody knows where it come from
Holding everything and everything
From the darkest fantasy
To the unicorns
Every particle is alive
And can move
Different shapes and sizes
Are the bodies aligned with time
Fighting like woods in a woodstove
Everything is the part of the same energy
Division began from two, three and many More
Every different sound is unique as it 's whole
Lord please tell me my fault
I am too small and a real fool
Who tried to dig feelings with a temporary tool
And if there exists a paradox world
Someone is laughing like me
Smiling and crying like me

I wish my thoughts meet the same level and one level up
of that scary dream
My senses cannot sense the end of dark
These are always a good trap
Neither my mind can tell the
Power of the supreme
To see the beauty I must leave
My conscience, to feel that I am burning,
I must travel the time
And if you feel it with your heart
One energy one form
Is pulling us very slow
Nobody knows where we will be
So its better to in natural flow
The algorithm of the life
The never ending vibes
There are many different meanings
To which it all function alive
Birds cannot name the fusion of skies
But the rhythmic pattern in the music can change the
colours of our eyes
The light from various suns
Are the symbol of hope and rise
Mysteries are hidden in the caves
Cold winds always blow the mind
Minds are overly fed, where stomachs
Are burdened
Souls are not attuned, though
Animals laugh at men
For the conceitful sight

All the intellects get old
After suppressing the ultimate voice
Where hands get struck
Rolling the same old dice
All started limitless years ago
It is the only sin to imagine
What the universe looks like
What inside the paradise ?
Where lies the paradise ?

Verse 11

I am upto a dream
I live around a lot of fickle beams

My toys are different,
Every scene I see
My toys are silly,
I can just hang it on a tree
It is a city, a village or a world truly
My toys are vibrant
To my mind, I sell stocks for free

I am upto a dream
I live around a lot of fickle beams

Hey you,
You the master of a single play
I bought a ticket or got one
To pass my lonely day
But when the sun will set
I will need to rest
I eat, talk and eat
Just like your regular guest

Let it be the mountains
Let my ears be filled with urban screams

I do not mind having another round
Let me first consider a whole new team
'olly for those who wish to place their heads on a golden bed
I am upto a dream
I see narratives ahead

To my friend
My troubled part, with a system or a hired guide
am not the one who is willing to predict and stand near the same old tides
I strive for both chaos and totality
I hardly care about their fortune and brutality
My horses are fed as I am ready for a ride
I am upto a dream
And dreams are hard to decide

And then

I know, of course, I know
My tongue would be stiffed
As my skin is ripped
My heart is wretched
My mind is picked
Time and again I call my inner eyes
And I jump to the very next beam
And I jump to the very best gleam
I am upto a dream

And then

I am floating over the sky
Though, I still want to fly
Fly high and high and high
My wings are broken by my father
My feet are not fast enough
My heart is wrenched with all kinds of serious lies
And I still want to fly
Fly high and high and high

Yes it is a fear
Because I am afraid to lose my tears
All the strange things, time want me to bear
For all the real, beyond my mind's sphere
I just want to fly
Fly high and high and high

Even I see no one that above
Makes me understand, what is true love
Service for nothing but just to serve
To feel the whole universe in my nerve
And I want to see another sky
Fly high and high and high

Bonus

Welcome Richard ! Welcome to my baby home
The hypocrite on the radio gave an erratic
Peroration
The ceilings and walls have no decoration
Mostly the mirrors do not reveal the real faces
All are stinted with factual quotation
Yes I live here alone and keep on singing the songs
I lay on my rutted couch with five or six clocks around
I usually clean the floor when the bold come out of the
frying pan and I cook some musty food only when I can
n my wardrobe, you can see all kinds of colourful garbs and
I do not mind if you take these all, because I am
colourblind and even these do not fit me at all
My telephone rings very rare
Every time I pick the call they say,
" Sir is there anythings you can bear ?"
I do not know how to use other appliances as well
These all are from the future
I just move these from shelf to shelf
All the curtains are untoward to the windows
Please help me in finding keys of the door's lock
And do not lay on the bed otherwise
You would get a serious heatstroke
Every night the whole home glow
All the angels sit together to watch the outmoded shows

The refrigerator is restocked with all kinds of sweet and spicy food
Remember not to touch any flowerpot
You would not get a stable mood
Welcome Richard welcome to my baby home